Magellan's World

FOR ESTHER MANN,
WHO STEERED ME TO MAGELLAN

Editor: Elizabeth Mann
Design: Lesley Ehlers Design

Copyright © 2007 Mikaya Press
Illustrations copyright © Gregory Manchess
Map illustrations copyright © Jane Shasky

OTHER GREAT EXPLORERS BOOKS BY STUART WALDMAN
We Asked for Nothing: The Remarkable Journey of Cabeza de Vaca
The Last River: John Wesley Powell & The Colorado River Exploring Expedition

Library of Congress Cataloging-in-Publication Data

Waldman, Stuart, 1941-
  Magellan's world / by Stuart Waldman ; illustrations by Gregory Manchess.
    p. cm. — (A Great explorers book)
  Includes bibliographical references and index.
  ISBN 1-931414-19-X (alk. paper)
  1. Magalhães, Fernão de, d. 1521—Juvenile literature. 2. Explorers—Portugal—Juvenile
literature. 3. Voyages around the world—Juvenile literature. I. Manchess, Gregory, ill. II. Title.
G420.M2W35 2007
910.4'1092—dc22
[B]

                                  2007061211

Printed in China

A GREAT EXPLORERS BOOK

BY STUART WALDMAN

ILLUSTRATED BY GREGORY MANCHESS

MIKAYA PRESS

NEW YORK

he first European explorers sailed into the unknown with maps based on the work of a man who had been dead for 1,300 years.

Ptolemy, a 2nd-century Greek astronomer and geographer, created the earliest known map of the world. In some ways, he was ahead of his time. Although people had known that the earth was round for hundreds of years, Ptolemy was the first to attempt to show a round world on a flat page. His map also may have been the first to include longitude and latitude lines to measure distances.

Nevertheless, most of his map was wildly inaccurate. It showed just three continents and two oceans. The Atlantic was a thin sliver of water and there was no Pacific Ocean. Africa was so long it extended all the way to the bottom of the world. China was so wide it covered most of Asia and nearly half the earth.

While some continents were larger in Ptolemy's map, the earth itself was relatively small. Because the vast Pacific Ocean was missing, Ptolemy's world was thousands of miles smaller than the real world.

But people in the 15th century believed that the learning of the ancients was far superior to their own. They revered Ptolemy as a great scientist, and cartographers drew maps that repeated his errors.

By the beginning of 16th century, explorers were sailing to distant parts of the world. They planned expeditions using Ptolemy-inspired maps, and their already dangerous voyages became even more dangerous, and all too often, deadly.

This Ptolemaic map was created in 1494. Because of its elaborate style—15th century maps were works of art more than science—it's difficult to understand at first.

The blue on the left is the Atlantic Ocean ❶; the bottom blue is the Indian Ocean ❷. The top left area is Europe ❸, the tan area below it is Africa ❹, and most of the expanse of white on the right is China ❺. Compare it to our present-day map and you get a sense of how wrong Ptolemaic maps were.

Magellan

KEEP THE OTHER SIDE OF
THIS PAGE OPEN.

YOU CAN READ ABOUT
MAGELLAN'S TRAVELS
AND FOLLOW THEM ON
THE MAP AT THE SAME TIME.

THE ARMADA DE MOLUCCAS
September 20, 1519—September 6, 1522

OUTBOUND ROUTE — — — — — — —

RETURN ROUTE — — — — — — —

GREENLAND

NORTH AMERICA

EUROPE

SPAIN

PORTUGAL

CANARY ISLANDS

JAPAN

THE PHILIPPINES

INDIA

MALABAR COAST

CEYLON (SRI LANKA)

PACIFIC OCEAN

THE MOLUCCAS

AFRICA

CCA

SOUTH AMERICA

AUSTRALIA

RIO DE JANEIRO

ATLANTIC OCEAN

N

W E

S

PORT ST. JULIAN

STRAIT OF MAGELLAN

ANTARCTICA

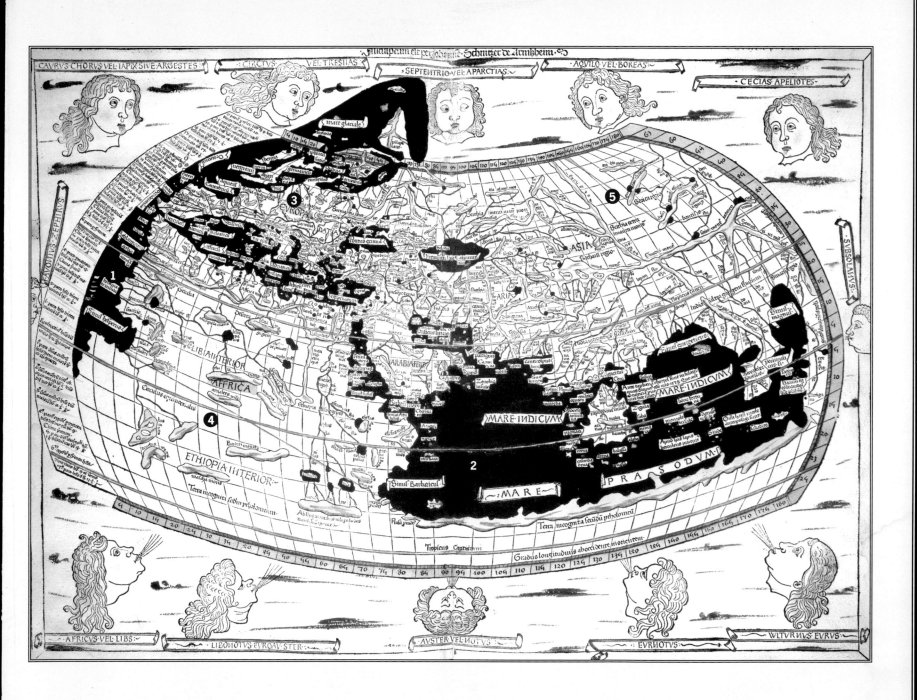

King Manuel I glared as Ferdinand Magellan limped into his court. The Portuguese king had never liked Magellan, but recently his dislike had turned to anger. Months before, Magellan had asked Manuel to support an expedition to the distant Molucca Islands and Manuel had turned him down. Refusing to accept his king's decision, Magellan returned to court three times with the same request. His stubborn persistence infuriated Manuel.

On this day in September of 1517, Magellan made no mention of the Moluccas. Instead, he asked for permission to leave Portugal and offer his services elsewhere. Relieved to be rid of him, Manuel told Magellan he could go where he liked. Magellan bent down on one knee and reached out to kiss the king's ring. Manuel turned his back on him.

A month later, Magellan crossed the border into Spain. King Manuel would never see him again, but he would hear of him.

If someone had told the young Ferdinand Magellan that he would one day leave Portugal and move to Spain, he would have laughed—or more likely drawn his sword.

Spain and Portugal were bitter rivals, and Magellan was a proud Portuguese, descended from a family of knights. In 1492, when he was twelve, his father sent him to the royal court in Lisbon where he was educated. Magellan studied traditional subjects like reading, writing and mathematics, but he also learned maritime skills like navigation and seamanship.

Portugal was a coastal nation and had always depended on the sea for its survival. In the early 15th century, Portuguese ships began exploring the long coast of Africa. As they sailed further and further south, Portuguese explorers learned that their maps were wrong: The African continent did not extend to the bottom of the world. The Portuguese believed that they could sail around the tip of Africa, and get to the southern part of Asia, or as Europeans called it, the Indies.

The Indies was the only place in the world where spices grew, and spices brought incredible wealth. Although it may seem difficult to believe now, a common spice like nutmeg was once worth as much as gold. Arab countries controlled all the land routes to the Indies, and for nearly 1,000 years, Arab merchants had made a fortune selling spices to Europeans. By sailing around Africa, Portugal would have its own route to this lucrative trade.

NUTMEG

European nobles were willing to pay almost any price for spices.

At a time when there was no refrigeration, spices were essential to hide the taste of rotting fish and meats. They were also important ingredients in perfumes and were thought to have miraculous healing powers. Medieval doctors recommended spices as a cure for everything from earaches and toothaches to arthritis, cancer, even the plague!

If you could afford spices, it meant that you were very rich. Some nobles bought spices for the same reason some people buy fancy jewelry and expensive cars today—to show off their wealth.

In 1499, the Portuguese explorer Vasco da Gama returned from a voyage around Africa with a cargo of spices. Portugal was in business.

From the beginning, Portugal's policy was to dominate the Indies and gain control the spice trade. Fleets of Portuguese warships bristling with cannons sailed around Africa. Small, lightly-armed Arab ships called dhows were no match for them. The wooden walls of Asian cities had no defense against them. One by one they fell: India's Malabar coast and its harvest of pepper; the island of Ceylon (now Sri Lanka) and its forests of cinnamon trees; Malacca, the rich Malaysian port city where native traders from around the Indies sold their cinnamon, ginger, pepper, nutmeg, mace and cloves. By 1511, little Portugal, a country smaller than the state of Indiana, had become one of the richest and most powerful nations on earth.

The money flowed to the royal family, to merchants and to those nobles who commanded expeditions to the Indies. Magellan yearned for wealth—his family was noble but not rich—but King Manuel appointed nobles he liked and trusted to lead expeditions. Ferdinand Magellan was not one of them.

In 1505, he joined an expedition to the Indies and set about proving his worth. Magellan turned out to be a born warrior—courageous, decisive and a natural leader. During a major battle at Malacca, he slashed his way through an armed mob and saved the lives of his captain and shipmates. Magellan fought in many battles and was wounded numerous times. Still, no matter what he accomplished, King Manuel never gave him command of an expedition.

In 1512, while serving in Malacca, Magellan received a letter that would change his life. It was from Francisco Serrão, a boyhood friend who had sailed with Magellan to the Indies. Months before, Serrão had been in command of a ship that hit a reef and sunk in the Indian Ocean. He survived and ended up on the island of Ternate, one of the small islands in the Molucca chain. Marrying a sultan's daughter, Serrão settled into a life of luxury. Carried by a native trading ship to Malacca, his letter to Magellan told of the fortune that could be made in the Moluccas.

The Moluccas were also called the Spice Islands by Europeans. Clove trees grew in the Moluccas and nowhere else in the world. Very close by were the equally small Banda Islands, or South Moluccas, where all the world's nutmeg trees grew. Because of their rarity, cloves, nutmeg and mace—made from the skin of the nutmeg's kernel—were the most valuable spices on earth!

The Moluccas were known to lie to the east of other Portuguese territories but no Portuguese expedition had reached them. In his letter, Serrão described the islands as being much farther east than had been thought. He said they were so far east that they were close to the New World.

Magellan became very interested in the Moluccas. He began thinking about leading an expedition to the islands. It would sail by a different route: not around Africa and east, but west to the New World.

Even after the discovery of the New World, cartographers continued to believe in Ptolemy's smaller earth.

In this drawing of a globe created in 1515, there is still no Pacific Ocean. Instead, Asia and the New World are separated by a small sea, making the Indies appear much closer to the New World than they actually are.

Since Serrão's letter located the Moluccas far to the east of the other Indies, Magellan concluded that they would be very near the coast of South America—about here (X).

In 1512, Magellan was still in the army and could do nothing about the Moluccas. Three years later, his fighting days were over and he returned to Lisbon. Magellan was then in his mid-thirties, middle-aged at a time when few people lived past sixty. He was also poorer than when he had left Portugal, having invested his money with a merchant who died without paying him back. All he had to show for a decade of service to his country was a severe limp from a knee that had been shattered in battle. The Moluccas were his last chance for the wealth and glory he craved. He began planning his expedition.

There was one large obstacle: the New World. Magellan had to figure a way to get his ships past it before he could reach the Moluccas. Ever since Columbus, cartographers had assumed that there must be a water passage, a strait, that cut through the New World. Different maps placed the strait in different places, but so far nobody had found it. Scouring dimly lit libraries for the latest maps and charts, consulting with Portugal's most brilliant geographers and navigators, Magellan turned himself into an expert on New World geography. By 1517, he had come to the conclusion that the strait was somewhere in the southern part of the New World. He believed he could find it and sail through it to the Moluccas. King Manuel disagreed.

And so, six months after leaving Portugal, Magellan stood before Charles I, the king of Spain. The sturdy, intelligent soldier impressed Charles, but he knew that Magellan's expedition, like any voyage of discovery, was a gamble at best. Magellan couldn't be certain his strait existed, and if it did, that he could find it. Even if everything went according to plan, there was no guarantee that Magellan would reach the Moluccas, or that he would make it back. Since the sinking of Columbus's ship the *Santa Maria* in 1492, more than 100 Spanish ships had gone down in violent storms, split apart on jagged reefs or simply vanished.

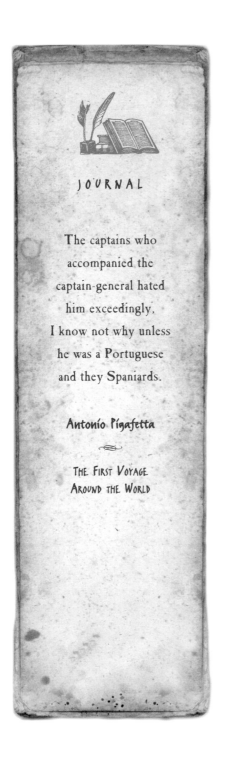

For King Manuel, who already controlled the spice trade, Magellan's expedition had not been worth the risk. For King Charles, who looked with envy at the money pouring into Manuel's treasury, it was well worth it.

On March 22, 1518 he gave Ferdinand Magellan command of a five-ship fleet called the Armada de Moluccas. He was named captain-general and given authority over every man in the expedition, as well as a significant share of the profits.

Magellan finally had the support of a king, but that didn't end his problems. In fact, it created new ones. The Spanish nobles who were to be Magellan's officers were outraged that they would have to take orders from a Portuguese. To them, Portugal was the enemy. Even a Portuguese who had left his country in disgrace was not to be trusted.

While the Spanish believed Magellan was still loyal to Portugal, the Portuguese thought him a traitor. His expedition threatened to end Portuguese control of the spice trade and increase Spain's wealth and power. King Charles had to assign bodyguards to protect Magellan because of rumors of Portuguese assassins.

It takes time to organize a large and complicated expedition. Because of the distrust, rivalries, threats and bickering, the Armada de Moluccas took even longer than usual. Magellan, with his single-minded intensity, persisted until finally, on September 20, 1519, the ships the *Trinidad*, the *San Antonio*, the *Concepción*, the *Victoria* and the *Santiago*, with 270 men aboard, sailed into the Atlantic toward the New World.

It was difficult to find sailors willing to sign up for such a long and dangerous voyage. Although Spanish officers would have liked the crew to be all Spaniards, in the end they had to accept men from many other countries. While the majority of the men were from Spain, over 100 sailors came from Portugal, France, Italy, Germany, Austria, Belgium, England, Ireland, Scandinavia, Africa, and India. It was the most diverse crew ever to sail on a voyage of discovery.

Six men didn't join willingly. They were slaves. Among them was Magellan's personal slave, Enrique, whom he had purchased in Malacca.

Each ship had small boats that were either hung on the side of the ship or towed behind it. The boats were used to carry messages between ships, land on beaches, or explore shallow waterways.

The ships were well-stocked with fresh water, wine, olive oil, vinegar, beans, lentils, garlic, flour, rice, cheese, honey, sugar, anchovies, and sardines, as well as codfish, beef, and pork preserved in salt. They also carried live cattle and pigs that were slaughtered during the voyage to provide fresh meat.

If the fleet ran out of food before reaching the Moluccas, there were chests filled with glass beads, bells, mirrors and knives to trade with native people for supplies. Chests containing expensive silks, linen and valuable iron tools were reserved for trading in the Moluccas.

The armada was well-stocked with weapons: 75 cannons, 100 full suits of armor, thousands of lances and swords, hundreds of crossbows and longbows, thousands of arrows, 50 primitive rifles called arquebuses, and dozens of barrels filled with gunpowder and lead.

The ships stopped in the Canary Islands to pick up their final supplies of water and fresh meat before sailing across the Atlantic. While in port, Magellan heard that Portuguese warships were out in the Atlantic, waiting to intercept the armada and arrest him.

Magellan ordered an immediate change in course. He knew the Portuguese would expect him to head in a westerly direction toward the New World, and that's where they would be waiting for him. So he sailed south.

The captain-general didn't tell his officers the reason for the change in course. All they knew was that they were no longer headed toward the New World. After several days, the *San Antonio*, commanded by Captain Juan de Cartagena, caught up with Magellan's ship, the *Trinidad*. Cartagena demanded to know why the armada had changed course. Magellan told him to obey orders and "ask no questions!"

There were good reasons for his brusque response. Juan de Cartagena was an arrogant young nobleman who believed he should have been appointed captain-general instead of a Portuguese. Back in Spain, Cartagena had been overheard discussing a takeover of the armada with Luis de Mendoza, captain of the *Victoria,* and Gaspar de Quesada, captain of the *Concepción*. Whether they were serious or not, Magellan had to establish that he was the captain-general and that he expected nothing less than unquestioned obedience from all his captains. Still, with no explanation, the change in course made the already suspicious Spanish officers even more suspicious. He was taking the armada down the coast of Africa, an area known for bad weather and unpredictable winds.

A few days later, black clouds gathered overhead. The waves rose and the sea crashed over the decks. The storms kept coming, one after another, with increasing fury and without a break.

When the storms ended, the sea turned dead calm—no wind at all. For three weeks, the Armada de Moluccas barely moved. Supplies were running low and sharks circled the ships.

The four captains met with Magellan aboard the *Trinidad*. Cartagena stood up and accused Magellan of trying to destroy the fleet because he secretly served the king of Portugal. Cartagena announced that he could no longer obey Magellan's orders.

Magellan sat quietly, saying nothing in his own defense. When Cartagena had finished speaking, he issued a command. Suddenly, three officers surrounded Cartagena with their swords drawn. Magellan stood up and drew his own sword. "Rebel, you are under arrest," he said. Cartagena turned to Captains Quesada and Mendoza and pleaded with them to attack Magellan. The two men looked at the captain-general and the armed officers and didn't move.

Magellan could have executed Cartagena for mutiny, but he was the son of one of Spain's most powerful nobles. Besides, Magellan believed he could afford to be generous. Having easily put down the mutiny, he was certain neither Cartagena, nor any other Spanish officer, would dare try again.

He ordered Cartagena to be brought to the main deck and, in front of the entire crew, the proud nobleman was placed in stocks as if he were a common thief. He was released the next day, and removed from command of the *San Antonio*. Magellan's cousin, Álvaro de Mesquita, became captain of the *San Antonio*. Now two ships had Portuguese captains. Spanish officers were not happy, but they could do nothing about it.

A few days later, the first breeze in weeks ruffled the *Trinidad*'s sails. Magellan, certain they were far south of the Portuguese warships, ordered a change in course—west to the New World!

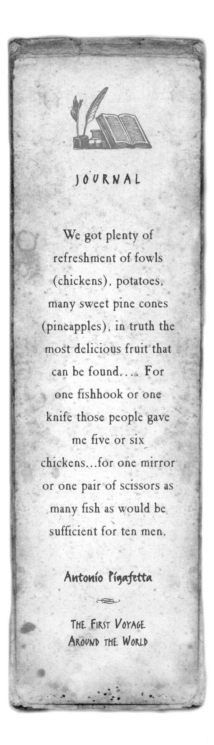
On December 13, the five ships sailed into the harbor of Rio de Janeiro, Brazil. They were immediately surrounded by canoes belonging to members of the Guaraní tribe. The men readied their weapons, but there was no need for them. The armada had arrived on the same morning that a rainfall ended a long drought. The Guaraní believed the ships were giant canoes sent by the gods to bring rain.

Magellan needed the Guaraní's friendship. The change in course and the bad weather had slowed the armada to the point where most of the food was gone. Magellan opened his chests of trinkets. The next day, Rio de Janeiro's palm-lined beaches became a marketplace where scissors were exchanged for geese, playing cards for chickens, and mirrors for fish. In a very short time, the armada was resupplied.

The crew returned to the beach nearly every day. They communicated with the Guaraní through sign language, particularly with the pretty young women. Magellan, a deeply religious man, was upset to see Christian men mix with heathen women, but his crew was exhausted and needed rest. He pushed aside his religious beliefs and allowed the men to go ashore. As for himself, he was all business, supervising repairs to the storm-battered ships and planning the most difficult part of the voyage—finding the strait.

Magellan believed it was south of Rio de Janeiro, but he was uncertain exactly how far south. The armada set sail the day after Christmas, and for the next three months, it probed the coastline of South America. They found coves and bays and rivers, but no strait.

Weather in the southern hemisphere is the reverse of ours: It gets colder as you go south. The armada sailed down the coast, and the weather turned first chilly, then cold, and finally brutally cold. On February 27, the men spotted a flock of black-and-white birds that waddled comically and never flew. The Spanish called them *patos sin alas*—wingless ducks. We call them penguins.

The armada was now closer to Antarctica than to Rio. Winter was approaching (seasons are also reversed in the southern hemisphere) and it would soon get even colder. There was still no sign of the strait. Many of the officers doubted that it existed, and some spoke of returning to Spain.

The ships sailed through a narrow passage into a broad bay. Surrounded by extremely high cliffs, the bay was sheltered from the worst of the icy polar winds. Magellan named it Port St. Julian and gave orders to drop anchor. The armada would remain in Port St. Julian through the winter and resume searching for the strait in the spring. It was now clear to all the officers: Ferdinand Magellan would never turn back.

Captains Mendoza, Quesada, and former captain Juan de Cartagena secretly met with other Spanish officers aboard the *Concepción*. The following night, a group of armed men led by Cartagena climbed into the *Concepción's* boat and rowed to the *San Antonio*. An hour later, Magellan's cousin was in chains and Cartagena was again in command.

In the morning, another boat pulled alongside the *Trinidad*. A rebel officer delivered a letter to Magellan. The rebels demanded that the ships return to Spain immediately. If not, they would take over the armada.

Magellan knew he was in trouble. He had command of only one other ship besides the *Trinidad*, the *Santiago,* whose captain was Spanish but had remained loyal to him. The *Santiago* was, by far, the smallest ship in the fleet. Magellan was outmanned and outgunned.

That night, a boat brought one of the *Trinidad's* officers, Gonzalo Gómez de Espinosa, to the *Victoria*. He carried a letter from Magellan to the *Victoria's* captain. As Mendoza read the letter, he shook his head in disbelief. Magellan was ordering him to surrender his ship. Mendoza crumpled the letter and threw it on the floor as if it were trash. Without any warning, Espinosa grabbed Mendoza by his hair, jerked his head back, pulled out a knife that was hidden in his shirt and slashed the captain's throat. As Mendoza slumped to the floor in a pool of blood, Espinosa calmly walked to the porthole and waved a lantern.

At the signal, another boat from the *Trinidad* pulled alongside the *Victoria*. Magellan's men swarmed aboard, and the shocked and leaderless rebel officers gave up. Magellan ordered the *Victoria*, the *Trinidad,* and the *Santiago* to sail to the mouth of the bay and block the escape route of the two remaining ships. The following day, the *Concepción* and *San Antonio* surrendered.

This time Magellan showed no mercy. Three rebel officers were tortured, one so brutally that he died from his ordeal. Because he had been a leader of the mutiny, Quesada was immediately executed. Both his and Mendoza's heads were stuck atop poles and planted on the shore, a grisly warning to all who would defy Magellan.

Juan de Cartagena met the cruelest end of all. A few months after the mutiny, Magellan put him ashore on a small island. He left him no firewood, and enough food to last for only a few months. Two weeks later, the armada hauled up its anchors and sailed out of Port St. Julian. Marooned, facing a slow death from cold and starvation, Cartagena fell to his knees and cried out for mercy. Magellan never looked back.

The search for the strait resumed, but with only four ships. The little *Santiago* had been torn apart during a winter storm. On October 21, 1520, the armada sailed into a waterway whose current flowed from the west. The water was salty which meant it was coming from a sea, not a river. After a week of sailing, the ships still had not reached the end of the waterway.

Magellan was hopeful, but he knew that even if they had found the strait, there was no guarantee they could get through it. The waterway was long, and it twisted and turned like a writhing snake. Channels branched in every direction. Each time a ship approached a channel, a decision had to be made. Sailing into the wrong one could take the ship into shallow water where rocks would rip into its wooden hull.

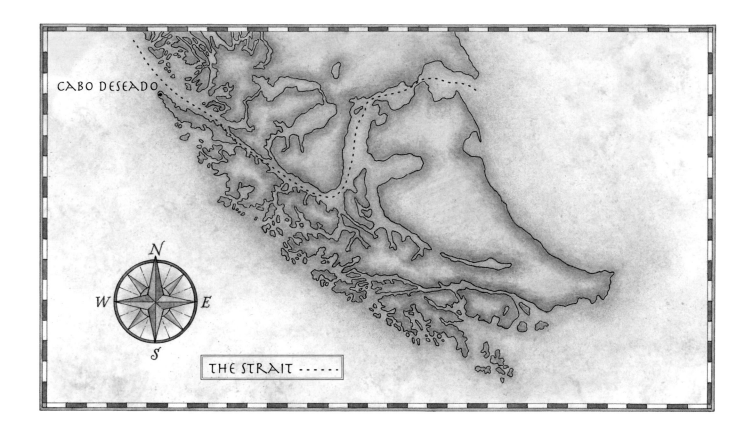

CABO DESEADO

N
W   E
S

THE STRAIT ‧‧‧‧‧‧

Navigating this dangerous, watery maze took all of Magellan's skill. He ordered lookouts to the tops of the masts where they had a bird's eye view of the waterway ahead. He sent boats ahead of the ships to explore the side channels. From time to time, the men in the boats would dip their hands in the water and taste it. If it was no longer salty, it meant they were no longer in the strait. The men would then return to their ships, and Magellan would plot the course based on their report. In this way, the armada slowly and carefully weaved its way through the strait.

One bright, clear morning a crewman from the *Trinidad* went ashore and climbed a 1,000 foot hill. In the distance, he saw the narrow strait flowing into open water. Waves pounded against the shore. It was the sea! When the crewman reported his discovery, Magellan burst into tears.

Magellan wanted to sail through the strait immediately, but one of the ships was missing. The week before, Magellan had sent the *San Antonio* to explore the southern part of the strait, and it had not returned. The three remaining ships searched the coves, inlets and channels along the strait. They fired their cannons, hoping for a response.They heard nothing. Fearing the worst, they peered into the water looking for sails, broken masts, shards of wood, any sign of wreckage. They saw nothing. The largest ship in the fleet seemed to have vanished.

The truth was much less mysterious. There had been another mutiny. Far from Magellan's watchful eyes, rebellious officers had taken control of the ship from Magellan's cousin. While the three ships were searching for the *San Antonio*, it was already out in the Atlantic on its way back to Spain.

The *San Antonio* had carried the bulk of the armada's supplies, and Magellan's officers were concerned by its loss. The captain-general, as usual, remained confident. Once through the strait, he was sure it would take a week or two at the most to reach the Moluccas.

On November 28, 1520, the *Trinidad,* the *Victoria* and the *Concepción* sailed out of the strait. Magellan named the last spit of land Cabo Deseado—Cape Desire, because he was soon to realize all his desires.

He was wrong.

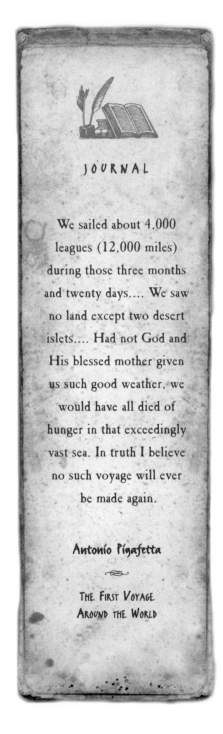

JOURNAL

We sailed about 4,000 leagues (12,000 miles) during those three months and twenty days…. We saw no land except two desert islets…. Had not God and His blessed mother given us such good weather, we would have all died of hunger in that exceedingly vast sea. In truth I believe no such voyage will ever be made again.

Antonio Pigafetta

THE FIRST VOYAGE
AROUND THE WORLD

By Christmas, the armada had been sailing nearly a month without sighting land, much less an island chain. Magellan now knew the worst: His maps were wrong. The Indies and the New World were not separated by a small sea, but by a very large ocean. He believed the Moluccas were somewhere on this ocean but he had no idea where they were or how he would find them. And yet, he gave no thought to turning back.

The armada sailed west, through January, February, and into March. Because there were no storms and the water was calm, Magellan named the new ocean the Pacific—after the Latin word for peaceful.

Aboard the three ships, there was anything but peace. The food was nearly gone. The little that remained was infested with maggots. The men roasted rats when they were lucky enough to find them. Otherwise, they ate sawdust and gnawed on leather.

Thirty men had come down scurvy—a horrifying disease caused by a lack of vitamin C. Their joints became brittle and painful. Their blood vessels burst and they bled internally. Their gums turned soft and their teeth fell out. Nineteen men died of scurvy and those that survived were weak and in severe pain. Their pitiful groans could be heard day and night.

At dawn on March 16, 1521, the *Trinidad*'s lookout squinted at a fog-shrouded shape in the water. As the ships moved closer, he could see the outline of an island. The fog lifted. There were islands everywhere! It was an archipelago, a chain so widespread and numerous that if all the islands were joined together it would be the size of a small country. Today we call this archipelago the Philippines.

Although the islands were unknown to Europeans, Arab and Asian ships had been visiting the Philippines for centuries. It was part of a trading network that stretched from China, to the Indies, all the way to Africa. When the native people of the small island of Limasawa saw the ships, they didn't think they were sent by the gods. They were just foreigners who might have something useful to trade.

A delegation from Limasawa's chief, Colambu, rowed out to welcome Magellan and invite him to a feast. Men who had been eating sawdust and rats were soon gorging on roast pig, rice, fish and deliciously sweet tropical fruits.

Magellan's interest was aroused by more than food. Limasawa seemed awash in gold. Meals were served on gold-rimmed plates. Colambu carried a gold-handled dagger and wore golden armbands and earrings. When he smiled, three gold dots glittered on each tooth!

Magellan set up tents for those ill with scurvy and fed them coconut milk with his own hands. The men slowly recovered thanks to the vitamin C in the tropical fruits, although nobody knew why they were getting better. The cause of the disease would not be known for another 250 years.

Magellan's slave, Enrique, turned out to have been born in the Philippines and spoke its languages. Magellan no longer had to communicate through primitive sign language. With Enrique translating, Colambu told Magellan of a larger, richer island than Limasawa—a trading center called Cebu. Magellan set sail.

Trading wasn't the only thing on Magellan's mind as he neared the island. Like the Portuguese, Spanish policy was to dominate countries and control the trade.

The ships fired their cannons, one after another, as they sailed into Cebu's harbor. On the beach, startled Cebuans gathered around the island's ruler, Humabon. They shook with each thunderous boom.

The *Trinidad's* boat landed on the beach. One of Magellan's officers, with Enrique translating, explained to Humabon that the cannons were the captain-general's way of saluting Cebu's ruler. Humabon was relieved. He may have even been flattered. But he was also frightened by the foreigner's powerful weapons—exactly what Magellan wanted.

A gold trader from Thailand also happened to be on Cebu's beach that morning. He told Humabon that the foreigners were the same people who had conquered Malacca and spread terror all over the Indies. Although the trader had confused the Spanish with the Portuguese, Humabon was thoroughly intimidated. He agreed to a treaty with Spain. A few days later, Magellan set up a trading post in the middle of Cebu.

Members of Humabon's court came aboard the *Trinidad* to swear friendship with Spain. Magellan dropped to his knees and thanked God for bringing the two countries together. The Cebuans, though not understanding a word, were fascinated at the sight of the fierce-looking, bearded foreign chief on his knees, shouting to the heavens. Magellan noticed their interest and spoke to the Cebuans about his religion. He urged them to become Christians and save their souls.

Spanish expeditions were expected to convert native people to Christianity. Magellan and the *Trinidad*'s priest, Father Valderrama, spread the word of their God to the Cebuans. King Charles had ordered that no native be converted by force, so Magellan assured the Cebuans that any person who didn't become Christian would live in peace. But, he added, those who did convert would receive special favors from King Charles.

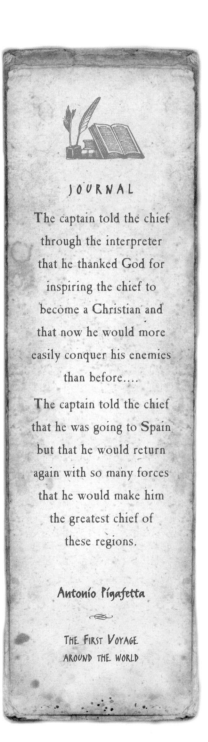

On Sunday morning, April 14, 1521, Ferdinand Magellan, dressed in the white robes of a holy man, strode onto a stage-like platform decorated with palm leaves and flanked by a large wooden cross. Both the cross and the platform had been built by Magellan's men the day before. With hundreds of his people watching, Chief Humabon converted to the Christian faith. He was given the Christian name Charles in honor of the Spanish king. Later that day, Father Valderrama baptized Humabon's mother, wife, daughter and members of his court. During the following week, 2,200 Cebuans followed their ruler and converted to Christianity.

Magellan had been in the Philippines a little over a month and had accomplished more than he could have ever hoped for. Without shedding a drop of blood, he had converted Cebu to Christianity and given Spain an important base in the Philippines. His men were recovering their health. His ships had been restocked with food and fresh water. Humabon had offered Cebuan pilots to guide Magellan to the Moluccas. It was time to set sail.

Magellan never gave the order.

Something had happened to Ferdinand Magellan after the Cebuans converted to Christianity. He began acting more like a missionary than a captain-general. Religion became his priority and the Moluccas were forgotten.

When Magellan learned that the Christian Cebuans continued to worship pagan gods, he warned that they would lose God's favor. He urged them to burn their idols. Incited by Magellan, rampaging mobs tore down shrines that had guarded Cebu's beaches for generations. Wooden idols were snatched from their owners' hands and tossed into bonfires. Cebu's old religion burned.

Magellan didn't limit his attentions to Cebu. He ordered a chief from the nearby island of Mactan to swear allegiance to Humabon as his Christian king—even though the chief had not become a Christian himself. When Chief Lapu Lapu refused, Magellan threatened to destroy his villages. Lapu Lapu sent a message to Cebu: His warriors would be waiting for Magellan. The captain-general readied for battle.

The armada's officers were shocked by what had happened. Juan Serrano, the former captain of the *Santiago,* who had remained loyal during the mutiny, confronted Magellan. They would be facing a large army, he said. Many men had already been lost through illness. If they lost more in battle, they might not have enough men to sail the ships. Their mission was the Moluccas, not Mactan.

But Magellan was eager for battle. He had told the Cebuans that one Christian soldier was worth a thousand heathens. Now he could prove it.

Serrano begged Magellan to at least remain aboard the ship during the battle. If the captain-general were to be killed, the armada would be leaderless. It was good advice, and it came from a man Magellan trusted, but he ignored it.

It was difficult for the men close to him to understand Magellan's actions; it's even harder for us today, five centuries later. Magellan had defied his king and left his country, battled mutineers, faced sickness and starvation, and had sailed half-way around the world to reach the Moluccas. Now that he was so close, why would he risk everything in a meaningless battle?

Historians have offered theories. Perhaps his success in converting the Cebuans had turned his religious fervor into fanaticism. Perhaps the years of hardship and anxiety had taken a toll, and he was no longer thinking clearly. In the end, we can only guess at what Magellan was thinking. All we can know is what happened that April morning on Mactan.

Forty-nine men piled out of two boats and waded toward the beach. 1,500 Mactan warriors emerged from the jungle, shaking spears and shouting war cries. The Europeans fired their arquebuses and crossbows, but their bullets and arrows landed harmlessly in the water. Magellan shouted to his men to cease firing until they were closer to the enemy. Possibly panicked at the size of the force facing them, the men kept on shooting until they were nearly out of ammunition.

When he reached the shore, Magellan unsheathed his sword and led the charge. Facing, for the first time, an armored enemy with metal swords and lances, the Mactan warriors retreated to a village just beyond the beach. Magellan's men followed them and threw torches into the huts. Infuriated at the sight of their homes burning before their eyes, Lapu Lapu and his men attacked.

The sky filled with spears and arrows. Most bounced off the armor, but a poison-tipped arrow pierced Magellan's leg. Now it was Magellan's turn to retreat. Slashing his sword in powerful arcs, he slowly backed toward the boats. Magellan fought for nearly an hour with all the fury and courage with which he had lived his life. Lapu Lapu's warriors were defending their homes and were just as furious and courageous. There were also many, many more of them.

When a spear slipped past his shield and drove through his arm, Magellan dropped his sword. Weakened from the poisoned arrow, helpless and surrounded, he sunk to the sand.

As Magellan's men fled to their boats, Lapu Lapu's warriors plunged their spears again and again into the blood-spattered body sprawled in the sand.

On April 26, 1521, Ferdinand Magellan died on a beach on the island of Mactan. He was 600 miles from the Moluccas.

agellan's defeat was a loss for Humabon as well. He had supported foreign soldiers and a foreign god. To regain the confidence of his people, Humabon turned on his former allies and launched a surprise attack. Nearly thirty officers and crewmen died.

After abandoning the badly leaking Concepción, the two remaining ships fled the Philippines and sailed to the Moluccas. They found the islands as rich as they had hoped. After a month, the holds of both ships were filled with precious cloves. The men made ready to return home.

Francisco Serrão had been wrong about the location of the Moluccas. The islands were not nearly as far east of Portuguese territories as he had believed. The quickest way back to Spain was the traditional Portuguese route from the Indies. The Victoria sailed around Africa, and on September 6, 1522, dropped anchor in the harbor of Sanlúcar de Barrameda, Spain. It had completed the first trip around the world!

The Trinidad wasn't as fortunate. After losing half its crew to scurvy, it was captured by a Portuguese warship. Most of the Trinidad's survivors died in prison. Including the mutineers who had returned on the San Antonio, only 90 out of the 270 who had left Spain three years before made it back home.

And what did all the suffering and death accomplish?

Despite the loss of three ships, the expedition made a profit from the 1,400 pounds of cloves the Victoria brought back to Spain. But King Charles wasn't interested in the profit from one expedition. He still wanted what he had sent Magellan to get: the Moluccas. Charles sent more expeditions through the strait, but they all ended in failure. The voyage was too long and the strait too treacherous. The Portuguese controlled the best route to the Moluccas, and in 1828, Spain gave up all claims to the islands.

The difficulties that later sailors had on the western route underlines Magellan's achievement. He had kept his reluctant officers and crew together by the force of his will. Refusing to turn back, he had led the armada through a 98-day, 13,000-mile ordeal across the uncharted Pacific Ocean. Perhaps his most remarkable feat was the passage through the strait. Magellan guided three unwieldy sailing ships with primitive navigational instruments through a 363-mile maze. The voyage through what is now known as the Strait of Magellan has been called the greatest navigational feat in history!

In the end though, Magellan's most lasting achievement had little to do with heroism, profits, glory or the ambitions of kings. The Armada de Moluccas gave the world something far more important: knowledge.

Ptolemy would no longer be a guide for cartographers. Maps of the world would be drawn from the testimony of men who had actually sailed around the world. These maps were not perfect. More lands were still to be discovered, and the accurate measurement of distances on the water wouldn't be developed for another 250 years. But the outline of the world, including the vast expanse of water that covered nearly a third of the earth's surface—the Pacific Ocean—was finally on the map.

Ptolemy's world had become Magellan's world—and the beginning of ours.

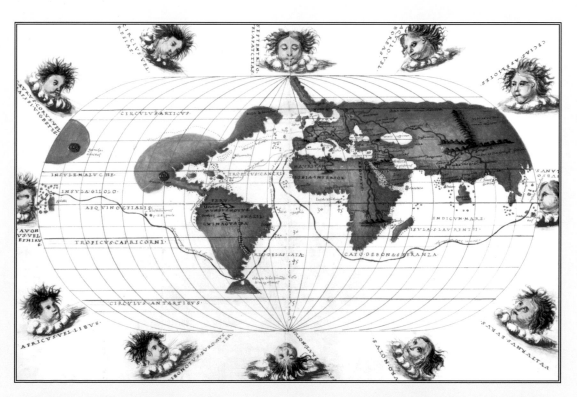

On his son Phillip's sixteenth birthday, a proud King Charles presented him with a map that traced the route of the Armada de Moluccas. Created only 20 years after Magellan's voyage, it bears a startling resemblance to the present-day world map.

SOURCES

Bergreen, Laurence, *Over the Edge of the World*, William Morrow: New York, 2003.

Joyner, Tim, *Magellan,* International Marine: Camden, 1994.

Morrison, Samuel Eliot, *The Great Explorers: The European Discovery of America*, Oxford University Press, New York, 1978.

Pigafetta, Antonio, *The First Voyage Around the World,* Marsilio Publishers: New York, 1995.

Russell-Wood, A.J.R, *The Portuguese Empire, 1415-1808*, Johns Hopkins University Press: Baltimore, 1998.

Thomas, Hugh, *Rivers of Gold: The Rise of the Spanish Empire from Columbus to Magellan,* Random House: New York, 2003.

Turner, Jack, *Spice: The History of a Temptation*, Alfred A. Knopf: New York, 2004.

Whitfield, Peter, *New Found Lands: Maps in the History of Exploration*, Routledge, New York, 1998.

Wilford, John Noble, *The Mapmakers,* Alfred A. Knopf: New York, 2000.

CREDITS

INDEX

AUTHOR'S NOTE

*The journal entries in this book are from the diary of Antonio Pigafetta, a young
Italian nobleman. Pigafetta was visiting the court of Charles I when he learned of the
Armada De Moluccas. The idea of a long and dangerous voyage of discovery appealed
to the adventurous Pigafetta and he signed on.
Since Magellan's logs were lost, and no other journal has survived, Pigafetta's detailed diary remains
the only day-by-day account of one of the most important voyages in history.*

ARTIST AT WORK

*From the initial sketch to the finished painting, Gregory Manchess shows the step-by-step
creation of the illustrations in* Magellan's World *at: www.Mikaya.com/artistatwork*